RE-INSTRUCT YOUR MIND FOR HAPPINESS AND SUCCESS

—

BY

DONALD K. LEAVENS

Disclaimer:

The information contained therein is for educational purpose only. It is not intended to replace professional advice.

TABLE OF CONTENTS

As a way of beginning this write- up, I want to you to consider these 4 questions.

1. Where does suicide come from?
2. What distinguishes a goal getter from a person with little or no motivation?
3. Why are some persons enthusiastic towards life while there are others that are unhappy?
4. Why do the rich stay richer? And those that are poor seems to lose the little that they have.

The answers to the questions above point to the functioning of the human mind. And the way you put your mind into use, the things that you allow into your mind, and the words that you eventually speak, all act together to determine the quality of life you have.

So, this book is written to show how best to make use of your mind.

It would also tell you some power words, which when spoken consistently, have the ability to push you from the place of self-defeat to the place of empowerment.

It is made of 7 power chapters that show that with a re-instructed mind, you are sure of a life of happiness and success.

Re-instructing your brain, often referred to as cognitive restructuring or cognitive retraining, can be a beneficial procedure for mental health improvement, cognitive improvement, and personal development. The following are some justifications for and instructions on how to retrain your brain:

Why you should re-instruct your brain.

To Change Your Negative Thought Patterns: People might acquire negative thought patterns over time that are detrimental to their wellbeing. By re-educating your brain, you can recognize these destructive thought patterns and swap them out for more beneficial ones.

To Enhanced Mental Health: As part of cognitive-behavioral treatment (CBT), cognitive retraining is frequently used to treat illnesses like depression, anxiety, and PTSD. You can lessen symptoms and enhance your mental health by addressing damaging or unreasonable thought patterns.

Improve Resilience through Growing: You can become more resilient in the face of difficulty if you have the ability to retrain your brain. You can overcome obstacles, control your stress, and overcome setbacks with its assistance.

Enhance Your Problem-Solving Skills: Cognitive re-training can help you become better at solving problems. You may improve your decision-making skills by pushing your brain to consider new ideas and potential solutions.

Enhance Learning: Re-educating your brain can speed up the learning process if you're seeking to learn new information or skills. It aids in the development of an open mind and a growth attitude.

How to re-instruct your brain

Practice self-awareness: To begin changing your mental patterns or beliefs, list them down. Be mindful of how these thoughts impact your feelings and actions.

Furthermore, **whenever you notice that you are considering a negative thought, challenge it**. Consider whether they are supported by facts or if they are overblown.

Positive thoughts should replace negative ones: Positive, realistic thoughts should be used to replace negative ones. If you frequently tell yourself, "I'm terrible at this," for instance, try telling yourself, "I may not be great at it now, but I can improve with practice."

In addition to the above, **become more mindful of your thoughts and emotions** by practicing mindfulness meditation. It can help you control your tension and anxiety.

Seek Professional Assistance: If you're having trouble retraining your brain on your own, think about getting assistance from a therapist or counselor. In this aspect, cognitive-behavioral therapy (CBT) is a systematic method that has the potential to be quite powerful.

Be gentle with yourself as you set realistic goals: Adapting to mental processes will take time.

You do not have to become too hard on yourself why trying to adapt to changes. And to avoid being too hard on yourself, you can do the following; talk with an affirmation, modify your working methods, energize yourself with positive thoughts rather than brutal force, set realistic goals and objectives.

Positive affirmations: Repetition of positive affirmations will help you build the new thought patterns you desire. Repeating encouraging phrases might gradually rewire your brain.

Some positive affirmations which you should speak to yourself on a daily basis are;

"I am prosperous."

"I have faith."

"I am strong."

"I am powerful."

"Every day I am growing better and better."

"Right now I have everything I need within."

"Motivated, I get up."

"I am a natural force that cannot be stopped."

"I am a wonderful example of motivation in action."

"I have plenty to live on."

"I'm leaving a lasting, uplifting impression on everyone I come into contact with."

"People are being inspired by my work."

Etc.

Consistency is crucial. Practice, practice, practice. Making changes to your brain's programming is a continuous process, so make it a routine to check in on and modify your thought processes.

Being consistent brings about internalization. This makes you to be able to apply knowledge or skills effortlessly.

Consistency also instills discipline. It is also used as checkpoints.

CHAPTER TWO

CHANGE YOUR BRAIN DIRECTION FOR SUCCESS

Your journey to success and pleasure may be impeded by a number of detrimental viewpoints and ideas. These viewpoints can stifle personal development, cause unneeded worry, and harm general wellbeing.

Here are a few examples of such detrimental ideas and viewpoints;

Perfectionism: Having the conviction that everything should be perfect can be crippling. It may cause worry, procrastination, and a persistent dread of failing. Progress requires accepting imperfection and taking lessons from errors.

Making Constant Comparisons to Others: Judgment, low self-esteem, and feelings of inadequacy can result from constantly comparing your accomplishments and enjoyment to those of others. Everyone's trip and circumstances are different from one another.

Overvaluing Material belongings: Having an unending desire for more might result from thinking that material wealth and belongings are the main measures of success and happiness. While having money is important, happiness doesn't come from it alone.

When you are materialistic, you place a high value on material possessions, and thus rely on your sense of self-worth and self-esteem on incentives and compliments from others. The idea that when goods become ours, they become more valuable to us than their value to other people is known as the endowment effect in behavioral economics. And such way of thinking may lead you to lose your true self and might cost you real success and happiness.

External Validation: Relying on other people's approval or societal norms for your sense of self-worth and pleasure can be harmful. True happiness frequently originates from within and is not reliant on the judgments of others.

All-or-Nothing Thinking: The cognitive error known as "all-or-nothing thinking" is frequently connected to depressive thoughts, anxiety, and low mood.

An unfounded thought pattern is referred to as a cognitive distortion. You might perceive things more pessimistically than they actually are.

The all-or-nothing fallacy entails seeing the world as two opposites, or binary, in nature. It is also referred to as polarized, dichotomous, or black-and-white thinking and is the propensity to view situations as "either/or."

As a result of the above, it can be demoralizing to think of happiness and success as two opposite possibilities.

Fixed Mindset: Holding onto the notion that your skills and intelligence are unchangeable attributes might impede personal development. Success can increase if you adopt a growth mentality, which views obstacles as chances to learn and develop.

Short-Term Gratification: Ignoring long-term objectives and concentrating just on the present pleasure might be detrimental.

Delaying gratification frequently results in more significant accomplishments.

Blaming Other People or External factors: Constantly blaming other people or external factors for your lack of success or happiness might leave you feeling helpless. For personal growth, accepting responsibility for your decisions and actions is essential.

In addition to the above, **burnout** can result from overcommitting and the belief that success necessitates persistently putting in long hours and forgoing one's personal well-being. Long-term satisfaction requires finding a positive work-life balance.

Neglecting Your Mental and Emotional Health: Your overall success and happiness may be hampered if your mental and emotional health is neglected. A fulfilling existence requires self-care, self-awareness, and the ability to ask for help when needed.

Setting Unrealistic Expectations: Setting excessively ambitious goals without taking into account your resources or limits can leave you disappointed. Setting difficult yet reachable objectives is more long-lasting.

Fear of Failure: Being excessively terrified of failing can prevent you from taking chances and experimenting with new things. Failure comes naturally during the learning process and can teach us important lessons.

Yes, the brain is absolutely essential to both happiness and success. While it's critical to recognize that success and happiness are complicated and diverse ideas influenced by a range of elements, such as heredity, environment, and personal circumstances, the functions and processes of the brain play a crucial role in these aspects of human life.

Let me quickly show you how the brain contributes to success and happiness:

Through cognitive skills: The brain is in charge of several cognitive processes, including reasoning, creativity, and problem-solving. These skills are necessary for succeeding in numerous facets of life whether they are in your work, relationships, or personal objectives in life.

Emotional Control: Neurotransmitters like serotonin and dopamine are released by the brain to control emotions. A healthy, balanced brain is better able to control negative emotions like stress and worry, which are essential for enjoying happiness.

Through setting goals and motivation: Motivation is greatly influenced by the brain's reward system. Your brain releases dopamine when you establish and execute goals, which encourages positive behavior and fosters a sense of accomplishment. Both success and happiness can result from this procedure.

Learning and Adaptation: The brain is remarkably adept at picking up new information and making adjustments in response to it. This capacity for flexibility can assist people in learning new skills, getting through obstacles, and eventually succeeding and being happy.

Through social ties: the human brain is wired for connection and social interaction. Positive social interactions and connections support satisfaction and can aid in achievement, particularly in endeavors requiring teamwork and collaboration.

Resilience: Brain function is directly linked to resilience, the capacity to recover from setbacks and adversity. A resilient brain can aid people in overcoming obstacles and disappointments on the road to success.

Positive Thinking: The brain can be taught to frame negative thoughts in a positive light. Positivity can improve one's ability to pursue achievement by lowering self-doubt and boosting confidence. It can also help one to be happier.

In your journey towards achieving success, there is a psychological method called "success reframing"; which entails altering how you understand and view success. It focuses on transforming your viewpoint from a constricting or pessimistic perspective on achievement to an upbeat and empowering one.

Let us see how success reframing operates:

The first thing is **to find limiting thoughts**. This means identifying any limiting or unfavorable thoughts you may have regarding success. Some examples of these presumptions are, "I'm not good enough," "I'll never succeed," or "Success is only for lucky people."

Once you've determined the source of these constricting ideas, confront them. Check to see if they are based on actual information or if they are merely conjectures. These beliefs frequently have no basis in reality.

Then **describe success for yourself:** Rather than relying on what others or society describe as success, define success for yourself. Your profession, relationships, personal growth, or any other part of your life could be involved.

Focus on growth and learning: Acknowledge that success involves more than just reaching a particular result. It also involves continued growth and learning. Consider setbacks and failures as chances for development and as stepping stones on the path to achievement.

In addition to the above, **set attainable objectives** by breaking down your long-term goals into more doable, shorter steps. Your drive and self-assurance can be increased by making realistic goals and acknowledging minor accomplishments along the way.

Change Your Attitude: Develop a growth mindset, which is the conviction that, with effort and commitment, you can improve your skills and intelligence.

 In the face of difficulties, this approach promotes tenacity and fortitude.

Then use **visualization techniques** to picture yourself succeeding in your chosen fields of effort. This may serve to further foster a successful mindset.

Surround yourself with positive influences: Spend time with those that encourage you to pursue your dreams. You can keep motivated and concentrated on your route to success with their support and positive energy.

Exercise Self-Compassion: Treat yourself nicely and accept that failures and setbacks are a normal part of any journey. You should treat yourself with the same empathy and consideration that you would extend to a friend going through a similar situation.

Keep trying: Success frequently takes time and effort. Remain dedicated to your goals and tenacious, and keep in mind that setbacks are temporary roadblocks.

Your chances of reaching your objectives and living a more happy life can be improved by changing the way you view success and embracing a more upbeat and growth-oriented mindset. Your ability to overcome challenges, take lessons from mistakes, and eventually achieve your desired degree of success can all be enhanced by success reframing.

A daily routine that is detrimental to your success and pleasure often consists of habits and actions that are ineffective or harmful to your general wellbeing. Here is an illustration of such a procedure:

Arriving Late: Arriving late can result in a hurried morning, which can ruin the remainder of the day.

Missing Breakfast: Missing breakfast might make you feel drained of energy and less focused for the rest of the morning.

Abuse of Social Media: Using social media excessively, especially in the morning, can be distracting and result in issues with comparison and low self-esteem.

Procrastination: Postponing significant duties and obligations can cause tension and anxiety when deadlines get near.

Lack of Exercise: excluding physical exercise from your day can result in health problems and low energy.

Unhealthy Eating Habits: Eating a lot of fast food or junk food can be bad for your physical and mental health.

Negative Self-Talk: Negative self-talk and self-criticism can undermine your self-esteem and general well-being.

Ignoring Personal Development: Skipping out on time for learning, developing personally, or following your passions can prevent you from achieving long-term success and satisfaction.

Poor Time Management: Being unproductive and feeling overwhelmed might result from failing to prioritize work and efficiently manage your time.

Neglecting Sleep: Consistently obtaining insufficient sleep can have a negative impact on your emotions, cognition, and general health.

Overworking: Burnout and decreased happiness can result from working too long hours without breaks or relaxation.

Refusing Social Connections: Refusing to interact with friends and family can make you feel lonely and unhappy.

Neglecting Mental Health: Long-term emotional issues can result from failing to address your mental health requirements and failing to get help when you need it.

Financial Irresponsibility: Not setting a budget or saving money can cause stress and volatility in your finances.

Lack of Gratitude: Negative thinking can be exacerbated by a failure to recognize and value the good things in your life.

Lack of Goal Setting: If you don't define clear goals and objectives, you may feel lost and unsatisfied.

Overusing screens before bed time: this can interfere with your ability to sleep. This includes using phones, computers, and TVs.

Skipping Relaxation Time: Not making time for leisure pursuits, hobbies, and entertainment can result in ongoing burnout and stress.

Ignoring Hydration: Not getting enough water can have an impact on both your physical and mental wellbeing.

Avoiding Reflection: Avoiding reflection can prevent you from growing personally and being more self-aware.

To build a healthier and more meaningful daily routine that adds to your overall success and happiness, it's critical to recognize such detrimental routines and make changes.

Creating everyday success habits can have a big impact on your long-term success and personal development. You can develop the following vital daily routines to lead a successful and joyful life:

Morning rituals: Get up early to avoid hurrying and start your day with plenty of time.

Exercise: Get moving to improve your health and energy levels. And also use breathing exercises and mindfulness practices to calm down and lessen stress.

Set objectives: Make explicit, definite goals. Set goals for the day and stick to them.

Prioritize your work: Choose the priorities and give them your full attention.

Management of time: Use a planner or calendar. Plan your day, set aside time for each task, and schedule it.

Time blocking: Assign distinct time blocks to work on related tasks in groups.

Do not multitask: To boost productivity and the caliber of your work, concentrate on one activity at once.

Schedule learning time: Every day, read, study, or pick up new information or abilities.

Always be curious develop a desire to learn and look for chances to draw from your experiences.

Eat healthfully: Keep a healthy diet to nourish both your body and mind.

Remain hydrated: Drink enough water throughout the day.

Regular exercise: Keep moving to enhance your mental and emotional wellness.

Positive Mentality: Consider your blessings while you work on being grateful.

Visualization: See your goals and success to stay motivated and focused.

Productivity methods: this include the following

i.   **Utilize task lists:** Make a list of chores, rank them in order of importance, and cross them off as you finish each one.

ii.   **Set due dates:** Set deadlines for projects to keep them seeming urgent.

iii.   **Take distractions away:** Keep distractions to a minimum and remain focused.

Building Relationships through Networking: this can be achieved through;

i. **Developing relationships:** Get in touch with coworkers, mentors, and friends who can help you achieve your goals.

ii. **Speak with people:** Keep in touch with people by calling or sending a message.

Take a break regularly: taking brief breaks can increase productivity and lessen mental exhaustion.

Practice deep breathing exercises: practice meditation, or do your favorite hobby as relaxation.

Review and Consider: A day's end review to reflect on your accomplishments, review what went well, and identify areas for growth.

Adapt and prepare: As you contemplate, change your plans for the following day.

Sleep and rest: Ensure you get enough rest: Make 7-9 hours of good sleep a priority each night to rejuvenate your body and mind.

Accept change: Be adaptable and willing to adjust your plans when unforeseen difficulties appear.

Learn from setbacks: Take use of failures as chances for development and education.

A vital fact to remember is that forming new habits takes time; thus, begin with a few that you find appealing and build them up gradually.

Also know that making these habits a part of your daily routine requires consistency, and they can have a big impact on your performance in both your personal and professional life over time.

Reprogramming your daily routine can help you grow personally, improve your wellbeing, and accomplish your objectives.

Here are a few factors why someone may want to think about reprogramming their everyday rituals and habits:

Goal Achievement: Reprogramming your life can assist you in prioritizing actions that result in success if your existing routines and habits are out of sync with your long-term objectives.

Increased Productivity: By improving your work habits, time management, and focus, changing your daily routines can result in an improvement in productivity.

Better Physical and Mental Wellness: Changing habits in relation to diet, exercise, sleep, and stress management can result in improved mental wellness.

Reducing Stress: You can enhance your general well-being by reprogramming your life to include mindfulness, relaxation methods, and stress-reduction practices.

Financial Stability: Managing your finances more successfully through budgeting, saving, and investing can lead to financial security.

In addition, **personal growth and development** can be promoted by establishing new learning habits, such as reading frequently or enrolling in classes.

Also, your **relationships can be strengthened** and made more enjoyable by altering communication habits and spending more time on interpersonal relationships.

Enhanced Creativity: You may increase your creativity and originality by changing your regular routines to include creative activities or practices.

Breaking Bad Habits: If you have bad habits or addictions that are preventing you from moving forward, reprogramming your life can assist.

When you reprogram your everyday life, you are **making time for joyful habits and hobbies**, which will lead to greater happiness.

Furthermore, by reprogramming your daily life**, it becomes easy to adapt to significant life events** or changes, such as beginning a new job, becoming a parent, or retiring.

Environmental Impact: Changing your lifestyle to incorporate more environmentally friendly practices will help you cut back on your carbon footprint and support environmental protection.

Cultural or Lifestyle Changes: Adapting to a new environment may need reprogramming whether moving to a new nation, embracing a foreign culture, or changing one's lifestyle significantly.

Personal fulfillment: You may experience a better sense of fulfillment and purpose if your everyday activities are in line with your passions and ideals.

Time management: By making the most use of the time you have available, you can achieve a better work-life balance and have more time for fun and relaxation.

Self-Discovery: You may go on a voyage of self-discovery while reprogramming your life, learning more about your genuine preferences, strengths, and weaknesses.

Breaking through Plateaus: When you feel stuck or in a rut, changing your daily routine might help you get through the point and re-energize your life.

Technology adaptation: As technology advances, you can stay current and competitive by modifying your daily routines to include new tools and techniques.

Crisis management: In times of emergency or crisis, rearranging your routine may be necessary to take care of pressing problems and needs.

Mental health: Making mental health a priority through counseling, meditation, or mindfulness exercises can be a strong justification for changing one's daily routine.

Your daily existence needs to be reprogrammed, and that requires self-awareness, commitment, and consistency. You should make a plan to progressively implement the adjustments you wish to make in the relevant areas of your life.

It's also advantageous to get aid when you need it from friends,

family, or specialists to help you make the appropriate changes.

Views that are harmful to your mental health can differ from person to person because what harms one person may not harm another in the same way.

However, the following are some typical viewpoints or thought patterns that may be harmful to mental health:

Negative Self-Talk: Constant self-criticism, self-doubt, or self-deprecating thoughts, can be detrimental to your self-esteem and general mental health.

Catastrophic Thinking: Constantly assuming the worst will happen in every circumstance can cause anxiety and ongoing tension.

Comparing Yourself To Others: Constantly evaluating your accomplishments, appearance, or way of life in comparison to others, can breed emotions of inferiority and resentment.

Perfectionism: Pursuing perfection in all facets of life can be draining and result in long-term tension and worry when unreasonable expectations are not satisfied.

Black-and-White Thinking: Having a rigid mindset and having a hard time coping with life's complexities are both caused by viewing circumstances in extreme terms (e.g., all good or all evil).

Self-blame: Your self-esteem and mental health may be harmed if you accept responsibility for circumstances that are out of your control or place the blame for them on yourself.

Rumination: Reflecting on mistakes made in the past or unfavorable experiences can result in depression and anxiety.

Dependence on External Validation: Feelings of uneasiness might result from a constant need for affirmation from others rather than respecting your own self-worth.

Victim Mentality: Constantly considering yourself to be the victim of external events might impede personal development and resilience.

Unrealistic Optimism: Optimism can be beneficial, but having an overly optimistic and unrealistic view might have negative consequences when expectations are not met by reality.

Extreme Pessimism: Constantly anticipating the worst without taking into account more unbiased perspectives can result in chronic negativity and hopelessness.

Stigmatizing Beliefs: Believing stigmatizing things about other people or about mental health problems can lead to prejudice and discrimination, which is bad for society as a whole as well as your own mental health.

It's crucial to keep in mind that occasionally experiencing unfavorable thoughts or views is a typical aspect of the human experience.

However, it could be advantageous to seek assistance from a therapist or counselor if these viewpoints start to persist, are skewed, or have a substantial negative influence on your mental health.

One method that can assist people in recognizing and challenging problematic thought patterns and forming healthy perspectives is cognitive-behavioral therapy (CBT).

Adapting your thinking to reflect a better view of your mental health is a demanding journey that is complicated and unique to each individual. To assist you in altering your thought habits, take into account the following steps:

Self-awareness: Start by becoming more conscious of the way you are thinking right now. Pay attention to the thoughts that come to you and try to spot any persistently bad or useless ones.

Choose the source: Try to comprehend the source of these thoughts. Are they a result of previous encounters, cultural pressures, or self-doubt? You can address them more successfully if you are aware of the cause.

You can also **challenge unhelpful or negative thoughts** as soon as you become aware of them. Examine your thoughts and determine whether they are founded on facts or assumptions. Replace them with logical and uplifting ideas.

Become more mindful: You can increase your awareness of your thoughts and feelings in the current moment by practicing mindfulness meditation. This awareness might aid in giving you more mental control and direction.

Cognitive-behavioral therapy (CBT): Think about getting in touch with a therapist who specializes in this type of treatment. CBT is a treatment strategy that concentrates on recognizing and altering unfavorable thought processes.

Affirmations: Use positive affirmations to strengthen more logical thought processes. To combat negativity, tell yourself encouraging things frequently.

By also **spending time with people who have a good attitude to life** to create a pleasant environment around you. People who are upbeat might affect your thinking and encourage you to adopt a more positive outlook.

Set attainable targets: Set attainable objectives to alter your thought patterns. Divide them into more manageable chunks, and acknowledge your achievements along the way.

More so, **read books, articles, or podcasts that encourage growth and positive thought** to educate yourself. Gaining knowledge and inspiration from others can be quite beneficial.

Make self-compassion a virtue: Treat yourself with kindness and gentleness.. Be kind to yourself as you would a buddy going through a similar situation.

Healthy lifestyle: A well-balanced diet, consistent exercise, and sufficient rest can all have a favorable effect on your way of thinking and general mental health.

Journaling: Write your ideas and feelings down in a journal. This can make it easier for you to spot trends and solve problems.

Ask for help: If you're having trouble, don't be afraid to ask for help from friends, family, or a mental health expert. They can offer helpful support and direction.

Before I go further, I want you to know that your whole well-being, including your success and happiness, are greatly influenced by your mental health.

Let me show you some key aspects of your life that are impacted by your mental health:

Productivity and Performance: Studies have shown that people who are in good mental health are more productive and perform better at work and in other spheres of their lives. You can concentrate better, make wiser choices, and effectively manage your time and duties when your mental health is in good shape.

Emotional Resilience: The emotional resiliency required to deal with life's obstacles is provided by mental health. It makes it simpler for you to recover from setbacks and carry on working toward your goals since it helps you deal with stress, difficulty, and setbacks.

Interpersonal Relationships: Stable relationships are a key component of good mental health. Being mentally healthy makes it easier for you to interact with people, empathize with them, and establish deep relationships. The key to happiness is having happy connections.

Confidence and self-worth: sound mental health might increase your confidence and sense of self. This can then result in more success and happiness since you'll be more motivated to seize chances and meet problems head-on.

Goal Achievement: Your capacity to set and attain goals is influenced by your mental health. Being mentally healthy can increase your motivation and persistence in pursuing your goals, which can give you a greater sense of satisfaction and accomplishment.

Physical Well-Being: There is a connection between mental and physical well-being. Your ability to prosper and find happiness may be hampered if you have physical or mental health issues.

On the other hand, maintaining excellent mental health can benefit physical health.

Innovation and creativity: A mind that is free from worries and negativity, is more likely to be imaginative and inventive in either artistic or business endeavors; and where thinking outside the box is required for success, having such a free mind can lead to increased satisfaction via self-expression.

Balanced work-life: Sustaining a healthy work-life balance is essential for long-term happiness; and this is made possible by having good mental health. Also, a having a balanced work life enables you to live life to the fullest, engage in hobbies, and spend quality time with loved ones, all of which can greatly enhance your general wellbeing.

Financial Stability: Your mental health may have an impact on it. Better financial judgment, professional advancement, and financial security are all benefits of good mental health, and they can all contribute to a happier, less stressful existence.

Quality of life: Ultimately, mental health greatly affects your general quality of life. A sense of purpose, fulfillment, and contentment are more likely to occur when you are in good mental health.

Your wellbeing may suffer by having a negative attitude regarding physical health.

This mentality frequently entails unfavorable attitudes, convictions, or actions that interfere with the pursuit of a healthy lifestyle.

 Here are some typical traits of a mindset that is detrimental to your physical health:

Lack of Motivation: People with a non-supportive mindset could find it difficult to find the drive to exercise or eat more healthfully. They could view eating well as being too constrictive and exercising as a nuisance.

Always engaging in negative self-talk: this means constantly criticizing oneself and holding the belief that one cannot reach their fitness and health goals. This mentality can undermine self-assurance and make it challenging to maintain commitment to a better way of living.

All-or-Nothing Thinking: Some individuals with a negative outlook take an all-or-nothing stance on their health. They think there is no point in trying at all if they can't do things properly. This may cause healthy habits to come and go in cycles.

Procrastination: People who have an unsupportive mindset may put off taking steps to enhance their physical health. They could put off beginning an exercise program or changing their diet, frequently providing a variety of justifications.

Emotional Eating: Using food to deal with stress, sadness, or other emotions is known as emotional eating. Unsupportive people may choose unhealthy meals as a coping mechanism, which might undermine their efforts to achieve physical wellness.

Resistance to Change: Some people are wary of change and would rather stick to their unhealthy, ingrained routines. They can view changes in lifestyle as being too challenging or disruptive.

Comparison with Others: Comparing yourself to others all the time might make you feel inadequate and frustrated. When you notice that others seem to be having more success in their efforts to improve their health and fitness, you may become demoralized.

External Blame: People with an unsupportive mindset may place the blame for their poor health on external factors like genetics, time limits, or workplace stress rather than accepting responsibility for their own health decisions.

Lack of Knowledge: Because some people don't know what makes a healthy lifestyle, they may have an unsupportive mindset. This lack of knowledge may lead to unwise decisions and a reluctance to ask for help.

Low Self-Worth: A negative view of oneself might contribute to a negative mentality. People may not prioritize their health if they don't think they deserve it.

Quickly note that self-awareness, encouraging self-talk, setting realistic objectives, getting support from others, and gradually changing one's lifestyle are frequently used to overcome an unsupportive mindset toward physical health.

It's crucial to understand that each person's path to improved health is different, and it's acceptable to seek expert advice—for example, from a therapist or a nutritionist—if necessary. Although shifting one's perspective can be difficult, doing so is essential for obtaining and upholding a healthy lifestyle.

Let us now go over how to achieve a new perspective to your physical health.

They include;

1. **Holistic Well-Being:** Consider your physical health as a crucial component of your entire well-being rather than seeing it in isolation. Your mental, emotional, and social well-being are all linked to your physical health. In addition to nutrition and exercise, caring for your body also include stress management, building healthy relationships, and cultivating a good outlook.

2. Health at Every Size: Dispel the myth that health is only based on weight or outward appearance. The Health at Every Size (HAES) movement champions the idea that people of all physical shapes and sizes may engage in healthy habits and find happiness. Instead of aiming for a particular weight or body type, concentrate on how you feel and how you function.

3. Using Intuitive Eating: Ditch the rigid diets and calorie counting. Eating on instinct encourages you to pay attention to your body's natural signals of hunger and fullness. Choose foods that will satisfy both your physical and emotional needs, eat only when you are hungry, and stop eating when you are full.

4. Moment of Joy: Adopt physical activity as a source of joy and pleasure as opposed to using it only to manage your weight. Whatever you do, whether it's dancing, hiking, gardening, or playing a sport, find something you actually enjoy doing. When you exercise because you genuinely love it, it becomes a permanent fixture of your way of life.

5. Mind-Body Connection: Discover how closely your mind and body are connected. Yoga, tai chi, and meditation techniques help to improve not just one's physical flexibility and strength but also one's brain sharpness, emotional fortitude, and spiritual wellbeing.

6. Self-Compassion: Be compassionate with yourself when it comes to your physical well-being. Even when you make decisions that might not exactly support your health goals, be gentle to yourself. Over time, self-compassion can result in more favorable, enduring improvements.

7. Cultural Awareness: Be aware that cultural perspectives on physical health might differ significantly. The ways that different cultures approach nutrition, exercise, and overall wellbeing vary. Spend some time learning about and appreciating various viewpoints on health and wellness.

8. Rest and Recovery: Give rest and recovery top priority as vital elements of physical well-being. For physical and mental renewal, getting enough sleep and relaxing are essential.

Rather of adopting the "no pain, no gain" philosophy, pay attention to your body's signals to rest.

9. Environmental Considerations: Recognize how your way of life affects the environment. Environmentally friendly transportation, waste reduction, and sustainable dining can all improve both individual and planetary wellbeing.

10. Lifelong learning: Acknowledge the possibility that your perspective on physical health may change over time. Keep an open mind to new studies, fashions, and methods that fit with your principles and objectives. Continue learning and adjusting your strategy as necessary.

Before I proceed to another aspect of having a new perspective to your physical health, keep in mind that your view of physical health should be adaptable to your particular demands and situation. It's crucial to approach your journey to better health with curiosity and a willingness to try new things. What works for one person may not work for another.

Now, let us look at how adopting a holistic strategy that considers all facets of your lifestyle and well-being is necessary to achieve optimal physical health.

Below are some of the ways to preserve and advance physical health:

Consistent Exercise: Include a variety of workouts in your regimen that are balanced between flexibility, strength training, and aerobics.

When you are involved in regular exercise as the one suggested above, it keeps you in the right perspective about our physical health.

Go for a complete meal plan: By this I mean eat foods that are high in fruits, vegetables, whole grains, lean proteins, and healthy fats. Also, be mindful of how you consume processed meals, beverages filled with excess sugar, and avoid bad fats and sugars.

Keep Hydrated: To stay hydrated, sip copious amounts of water throughout the day. Drinks with plenty of sugar or calories should be avoided.

Also aim for **7-9 hours of good sleep each night** to get an adequate amount of rest. Make sleep a top priority and establish a calming night time routine.

Stress management: To effectively manage stress, practice stress-reduction methods like meditation, deep breathing, yoga, or mindfulness. Physical health can be negatively impacted by long-term stress.

You should also make it a habit to **visit your healthcare practitioner frequently** for checkups and screenings to maintain good health. To maintain healthy health, early detection and prevention are essential.

Maintain a Healthy Weight: Achieve and maintain a healthy body weight through a combination of nutrition and exercise. Consult a healthcare professional to discover the weight range that is healthy for your body.

And lastly, alcohol and tobacco consumption should be kept to a minimum. Avoid using any tobacco products at all costs because they are harmful to your health.

Numerous advantages might result from changing one's view on reality, both personally and for society as a whole.

Several benefits are as follows:

Enhanced Problem Solving ability: Having a new viewpoint enables you to consider issues and challenges from several perspectives, which may result in more creative and efficient solutions.

Increased Creativity: By exposing you to various viewpoints, cultures, and ways of thinking, new perspectives can inspire creativity. In the creative industries like invention, design, and the arts, this can be very helpful.

Better Decision Making: Having a broader perspective on reality can help you make better choices. You can make more well-rounded and logical decisions by taking into account a variety of views and options.

Greater Empathy: Understanding and empathy can grow when we see the world from another person's perspective. It facilitates connection to others more effectively and could lessen bigotry and prejudice.

Another benefit is **exploring different viewpoints.** This can be a stimulus for personal development and self-discovery. Your beliefs may be questioned, which will motivate you to grow and change.

Conflict Resolution: Taking into account many points of view might result in more constructive and peaceful settlements to conflicts or disagreements. It enables parties to reach agreements and concessions.

Enhanced Communication: This is another benefit of having a new perspective to reality. With this, you can interact effectively and your views can be communicated to wider audience more clearly. All these become achievable aiming towards having understanding of various viewpoints.

Cultural appreciation: Seeking to have a new perspective to reality leads you to appreciate various cultures. And this causes you to become exposed to various cultures and customs, thereby gaining a fresh perspective on reality. This may result in a greater understanding of and respect for variety.

Innovation and Progress: New perspectives on issues or phenomena often lead to scientific discoveries and advances. Progress can be sped up in many areas with a new viewpoint.

Reduced worry and Anxiety: On occasion, our viewpoint on reality may be constricting and cause unneeded worry and anxiety. You may experience more peace of mind if you can realize that some of your concerns are unjustified thanks to a fresh viewpoint.

Adaptability: In a world that is changing quickly, being receptive to new ideas might help you become more flexible. You're more prone to welcome change and deal with uncertainty skillfully.

Global Awareness: It is essential to comprehend many viewpoints on international issues in today's interconnected globe. It enables ethical and informed global citizenship.

Improved Relationships: In both personal and professional relationships, taking into account other viewpoints can lead to greater friendships, improved communication, and fewer disputes.

Opportunities for Learning: Taking on different viewpoints might increase your curiosity and willingness to learn. You're more inclined to look for novel encounters and educational experiences.

Personal Fulfillment: As you develop intellectually and emotionally, exploring many points of view can improve your life and give you a sense of fulfillment and purpose.

To wrap up the preceding concepts, adopting a fresh viewpoint on reality can be a life-changing and gratifying experience. In the end, it can help both individuals and society as a whole by fostering personal growth, bettering problem-solving skills, and increasing empathy.

Having a new perspective is becoming more important due to the benefits it offers.

Here are some actions to take in order to change your perspective:

Develop Curiosity: Live with a curious attitude. Speculate on the world, individuals, and current events. Be willing to consider many theories and points of view.

Read widely to broaden your knowledge: Read a variety of books, articles, and essays. Add a variety of genres, cultures, and points of view to your reading list.

Travel: You can encounter different cultures, traditions, and lifestyles through travel. It enables you to obtain a wider perspective and perceive the world from a different position.

You can also **talk to people who have various perspectives, histories, and experiences** to engage in dialogue. Even if you don't agree with their opinions, pay attention and make an effort to comprehend them.

Question Your Presumptions: Think about your presumptions and ideas. Are there any prejudices or biases that might be limiting your viewpoint? Be willing to adapt and to challenge them.

Learn from a Variety of Sources: Look for knowledge and information from a range of sources, including some that might contradict your preexisting beliefs. This enables you to consider various viewpoints on a subject.

More so, **practice empathy** by putting oneself in others' situations and making an effort to comprehend their emotions, ideas, and experiences. You may become more sympathetic and understanding as a result.

You can also **consider spending some time in meditation and reflection**. You may be able to see things differently as a result of gaining understanding of your own ideas and feelings.

Another way to gain a new perspective to reality is to **step out of the things you have become used to by reaching towards new hobbies or interests.** This produces fresh experiences. Your horizons can be expanded through new experiences, which can also provide you new insights.

Request Feedback: Consult with mentors or trustworthy friends for their opinions. They might provide information or viewpoints that you hadn't thought of.

Studying history will help you understand how societies, cultures, and ideas have changed over time. This can give important background information for comprehending the present. This is another way to have a new perspective towards reality.

Furthermore, **Practice mindfulness to see things more clearly and without prejudice or bias**. Being mindful of the moment can help you see things more clearly and without prejudice or bias.

Also **keep up with current affairs and international concerns to stay informed**. You can gain more insight into the world's potential and difficulties by becoming more aware of them.

Be Open to Change: Stay flexible in your own life. Sometimes accepting change and moving outside of your comfort zone will lead to personal development and a fresh viewpoint.

Learn from Others: Pay attention to other people's experiences and stories. Personal narratives can offer insightful perspectives on a variety of facets of life.

In conclusion, keep in mind that changing your perspective is a continuous process. It calls for an open mind, a desire to learn, and the humility to acknowledge that your viewpoint might change with time. If you embrace the process of personal growth and discovery, you'll continue to build a more complex and nuanced perspective on the world.

The idea that the mind has the power to heal is one that is frequently connected to several types of complementary and alternative medicine, as well as some facets of psychology and mind-body medicine.

The fundamental tenet of it is that a person's mental and emotional health can have a major influence on their physical wellbeing and capacity to recover from disease or injury.

Here are some important factors to think about:

The Placebo effect: This is a well-known occurrence in which a patient feels as though their condition has improved after receiving a treatment that has no therapeutic benefit. The person's confidence in the effectiveness of the treatment and their optimistic expectations are credited with this progress. It emphasizes how influential the mind can be on the healing process.

Mind-Body Connection: Many supporters of mind-body medicine hold that the mind and body are intertwined and that feelings, ideas, and beliefs can have an impact on one's physical well-being. For instance, stress is frequently mentioned as a component that might contribute to the onset or worsening of a number of medical disorders.

Meditation and visualization are another two healing modalities that encourage people to utilize their minds to aid in their own healing. These modalities include guided imagery, meditation, and mindfulness. People frequently use visualization techniques, in which they picture themselves in a healthy state or the body's normal healing processes.

Reducing Stress: Chronic stress has been related to a number of health problems, such as heart disease, digestive problems, and impaired immune system. Learn how to control your stress through breathing exercises, cognitive behavioral therapy, or other strategies.

Emotional stability and positive thinking: Keeping a positive outlook and feeling emotionally stable might be beneficial to general health. A positive outlook and a solid support network can help people cope with illness and may even speed up the body's ability to recover.

Furthermore, **therapies based on mindfulness include mindfulness-based stress reduction (MBSR) and mindfulness-based cognitive therapy (MBCT),** which use mindfulness practices to help people manage discomfort, lessen the symptoms of certain illnesses, and enhance their general well-being.

And lastly, both **biofeedback and neurofeedback** entail observing physiological processes, such as heart rate or brainwave patterns, and giving the patient feedback. Individuals may be able to affect their own healing processes by increasing their awareness of and mastery over these functions.

It's crucial to remember that while the mind can contribute to healing and wellbeing, it cannot take the place of necessary medical care. The power of the mind to heal should be viewed as a supplement to traditional medical practices. For the correct diagnosis and treatment of medical disorders, always consult with medical professionals.

Additionally, there is scientific research being done in this area to better understand the mechanisms at play because the efficacy of mind-based healing techniques might differ from person to person.

Let me also show you another dynamic of the mind in the area of achieving goals.

The power of mentality or the impact of one's psychological attitude on accomplishing goals and feats are other terms frequently used to describe the capacity of the mind to produce achievement. Positive psychology and self-help literature are both intimately related to this idea.

Key elements of how the mind might affect success include the following:

Positive Mentality: Retaining a positive outlook can significantly influence one's capacity for success. When people have confidence in themselves, they are more willing to take chances, persevere through difficulties, and perceive opportunities when others would only see barriers.

Setting goals: By establishing precise, measurable objectives, the mind may produce success. Your mind can direct its energy and attention toward realizing your objective when you have a clear target in sight, increasing the likelihood that it will happen.

Visualization: Visualization techniques entail imagining your intended results in your mind. Consistently visualizing achievement and imagining yourself accomplishing your objectives can inspire you and make accomplishment feel more satisfying.

Self-confidence: Self-confidence is a strong force. People are more willing to act, pursue opportunities, and endure in the face of disappointments when they have faith in their own skills.

Resilience: The capacity to overcome difficulty or failure is essential for success. People who have a resilient mindset can keep moving forward by seeing setbacks as opportunities for growth.

Positive Affirmations: Repeating positive affirmations or mantras can help reprogram the mind for success. By reinforcing positive beliefs about oneself and one's abilities, individuals can build self-esteem and confidence.

Mindfulness and Focus: Being mindful and present in the moment can improve focus and productivity, which are essential for achieving success. A cluttered or distracted mind can hinder progress.

Learning and Adaptation: Success can be increased by having a growth mindset, which is the conviction that aptitudes and intelligence can be improved via work and education. Taking on challenges and looking for growth chances can be effective strategies for success.

Another key aspect is **understanding and controlling one's emotions** as well as relating to others skillfully. This can help one succeed in both personal and professional relationships.

Leadership and teamwork are significantly influenced by emotional intelligence.

Grit and Persistence: Successful people have the willpower to press on in the face of challenges or hurdles. Long-term success may result from this grit, often known as mental toughness.

When it comes to generate wealth, the mind is a prominent tool to turn to. This is because the concept of the mind's capacity to generate wealth is intricate and varied, entailing a number of cognitive and psychological elements.

Below are few important factors to think about on how the mind does it.

Innovation and creativity: The human intellect is capable of coming up with original solutions to issues. This creativity can be used in business strategy, product development, and entrepreneurship, all of which can result in the generation of wealth.

Entrepreneurial attitude: An entrepreneurial attitude is frequently necessary for successful wealth generation. Entrepreneurs are prepared to take measured risks, spot market possibilities, and devote time and money to developing and growing their enterprises.

Financial literacy: Building money requires a solid grasp of financial concepts and techniques. Effective budgeting, saving, and debt management skills are included in this.

Goal-setting and planning: It's crucial to be able to establish specific financial goals and create a plan of attack to meet those goals. This comprises establishing both short- and long-term financial goals and tracking advancement toward them on a regular basis.

Resilience and perseverance: Getting rich typically requires overcoming obstacles and disappointments. Even in the midst of adversity, maintaining a positive attitude and working toward financial success are essential.

Education and Lifelong Learning: The capacity of the mind to learn new things and develop new abilities is essential for generating wealth. A competitive edge can be gained by keeping up with market trends, industry advancements, and emerging technology.

For the mind to generate wealth, **understanding and controlling one's emotions,** together with interpersonal abilities need to be in place. This is crucial for establishing and keeping good business partnerships, which can help to create money.

Also, learning **effective resource management** is essential. This includes managing time, money, and human capital.

This entails selecting sensible investments, maximizing effectiveness, and utilizing resources effectively.

To add to the key facts above, **building a strong network of connections and working together with others** can create opportunities for partnerships, joint ventures, and access to beneficial resources, which can lead to the production of wealth.

Even though the mind has a powerful capacity for money creation, it's crucial to understand that personal circumstances, outside variables, and access to opportunities can all have a huge impact on wealth generation.

A person's success and happiness are not just determined by their ability to accumulate riches, hence it is important to take other life goals and values into account when pursuing material success.